# The Man Who Saved Me

### Robert S Strong II

# Copyright

# Table of Contents

# Dedication

This book is dedicated to all those who have walked through the valleys of despair, searching for a light in the darkness. May this story inspire you to know that hope is always possible and that, even in the darkest moments, God's love and grace are waiting to embrace you.

# Introduction

You may be reading this because you are wrestling with your own inner demons, facing challenges that seem insurmountable, or struggling to find meaning in a world that often feels cold and unforgiving. Perhaps you've been betrayed by loved ones, lost a loved one to death, or suffered through the pain of addiction or mental health issues. Maybe you've felt the weight of your own mistakes bearing down on you, leaving you feeling hopeless and lost.

You may be questioning your own faith, wondering if God is truly there, listening to your cries for help. Whatever your struggle may be, I want you to know that you are not alone. Millions of people around the world are grappling with similar challenges, seeking solace and a path toward healing. This book is a journey of hope, a testament to the power of God's love to transform even the darkest of hearts. It's a story of overcoming the abyss of despair and finding a way to rise above the ashes of a broken past.

As you read through these pages, I invite you to open your heart to the possibility of change. Let my story be a beacon of light, illuminating the path toward a life filled with purpose, meaning, and the unwavering love of our Savior. This is not a story of perfection but a story of grace. It's a story of a broken man who found redemption in the arms of a loving God and a story that holds the promise of hope for anyone who is willing to believe.

# The Ongoing Battle

The journey of faith and recovery is not a straight line. It's a winding path filled with unexpected twists and turns, moments of joy and exhilaration, and yes, even moments of struggle and temptation. It's a journey where you might feel like you're taking two steps forward and one step back, constantly testing your limits and pushing you to your breaking point. But that's the beauty of it. It's in those moments of struggle, in the depths of our vulnerability, that we truly discover the depths of God's grace and the unwavering strength that comes from relying on His love. Remember, faith is not about erasing the darkness; it's about learning to walk through it with a light that shines brighter than anything else.

The battles we face may seem insurmountable, the temptations overwhelming, but we have a powerful ally by our side—the Holy Spirit, who whispers words of encouragement, empowers us to resist temptation, and offers us the strength to keep moving forward. We may stumble and fall, but we're not meant to stay there. We're meant to rise, brush ourselves off, and keep pressing on. I know what it's like to feel like you're on the verge of giving up, as if the weight of the world is pressing down on you, threatening to suffocate you.

I've been there, in that dark place where hope feels like a distant flicker, a faint ember threatening to extinguish. But I also know that even in the deepest darkness, God's light can shine through. He is the one who holds our hand through the storm, who whispers words of comfort when we feel like we're drowning in despair. He is the one who offers us the grace to forgive ourselves and others, and the strength to face our demons head-on. The journey of faith and recovery is a journey of transformation. It's about shedding the old, embracing the new, and allowing God to mold us into the people He intended us to be. It's a process that often involves facing painful truths, confronting our fears, and letting go of the things that hold us back.

But it's also a journey of immense joy, of discovering our true selves, and of experiencing the boundless love of God. We are not alone on this journey. We have a community of believers who stand with us, offering support and encouragement, reminding us of the love that surrounds us. We have the Scriptures, the living Word of God, to guide our steps, offer comfort, and equip us to navigate life's challenges. And most importantly, we have the Holy Spirit, who resides within us, empowering us to live lives of faith, love, and purpose. There will be times when the battle feels like it's too much to bear, times when the temptation to give up is almost irresistible.

But don't be discouraged. Remember the promise of God: "I will never leave you nor forsake you." He is always with us, even in the darkest moments. He is our constant companion, our unwavering strength, and our source of enduring hope. So let us continue on this journey, walking with God, holding onto His promises, and embracing the love He so freely offers. Let us not be afraid of the struggles, the temptations, or the uncertainties that lie ahead. Let us remember that God is with us every step of the way, guiding our path, strengthening our hearts, and lighting our way. The journey may be challenging, but the destination is worth it. It's a destination of joy, peace, and fulfillment, where we find our true purpose, our deepest identity, and the boundless love of our Heavenly Father.

# The Anchor of Hope

Faith, for me, became the anchor that kept me tethered to a life worth living, even when the storm raged around me. It wasn't a sudden, magical transformation; it was a gradual process of clinging to the promise of a better tomorrow, a tomorrow where the darkness wouldn't consume me. Before my encounter with Jesus, my world felt chaotic and uncertain. It was like being adrift in a sea of despair, with no compass to guide me and no land in sight. I had lost my sense of purpose, my belief in a future filled with hope and joy. Every day felt like a struggle, a constant battle against the overwhelming darkness that seemed to permeate every aspect of my existence.

But when I finally surrendered to the possibility of something greater, something beyond my own limited understanding, a glimmer of hope began to penetrate the gloom. It wasn't an instantaneous miracle, but rather a gentle, persistent nudging, whispering promises of healing and redemption. It felt like a lifeline thrown to me from a distant shore, a sign that I wasn't alone in my struggles. Faith, in its purest form, isn't about blind belief; it's about a deep, abiding trust in something larger than ourselves. It's about holding onto the promise of a future where love, forgiveness, and redemption are possible, even when the present feels bleak.

As I began to embrace this newfound faith, my perspective slowly started to shift. The darkness that had once engulfed me began to recede, replaced by a glimmer of light. I started to see the world with new eyes, recognizing the beauty and the hope that had always been there, even when I couldn't see it. Faith offered a new lens through which to view my past, my present, and my future. It wasn't about erasing the pain or the mistakes I had made, but about understanding them within a larger narrative of God's love and grace. It was about acknowledging that even in the darkest moments, God was with me, offering comfort and strength. It was a faith that wasn't simply a belief in a distant deity but a living, breathing relationship with a God who loved me unconditionally.

It was a faith that wasn't about rigid rules or legalistic pronouncements but about a deep, personal connection with a loving Father who sought to restore my soul. This faith became my anchor in the storm, the steady presence that kept me grounded when the world felt like it was spinning out of control. It wasn't about escaping the struggles of life but about facing them with a newfound strength and resilience that only God could provide. I learned that faith wasn't a destination but a journey, a constant process of seeking, growing, and surrendering to a power greater than myself. It was about trusting in the promises of God, even when I couldn't see the path ahead.

It was about embracing the unknown, knowing that God was always with me, guiding my steps and lighting my way. Faith, I realized, wasn't just about my own personal salvation, but about a desire to share the hope and redemption that had been given to me. It became a call to action, a burning desire to reach out to others who were struggling, to offer them the same lifeline that had saved me. My journey of faith was far from easy. There were times when doubt crept in, when the weight of my past threatened to drag me back into the abyss. But even in those moments, I held fast to the anchor of hope, knowing that God was faithful and His promises would never fail.

I learned that true faith is not about avoiding pain or hardship, but about enduring them with the knowledge that God is with us, carrying us through the darkest of storms. It's about finding strength and resilience in the midst of adversity, knowing that we are not alone and that there is always hope on the horizon.

The anchor of hope, forged in the fires of my own struggles, became the foundation upon which I built my life. It's the foundation upon which I continue to stand, even when the waves of life threaten to wash me away. It's the foundation upon which I continue to reach out to others, offering them the same lifeline of hope that was extended to me in my darkest hour. Faith is a journey, a lifelong pursuit of something greater than ourselves. It's about clinging to the promise of a better tomorrow, a tomorrow where hope triumphs over despair, love conquers fear, and redemption becomes a reality.

It's about trusting in a God who loves us unconditionally, who offers forgiveness and grace, and who desires to walk alongside us through every storm. And it's a journey that is worth taking, no matter how difficult the path may seem, because the anchor of hope, the promise of redemption, and the love of God are worth everything.

# Facing the Shadows

Surrounded by this loving community, I found the courage to dig deeper into my faith. I began to study the Scriptures, seeking guidance and wisdom from the words of the prophets, the apostles, and Jesus Himself. I learned about the power of forgiveness, the importance of redemption, and the boundless love of God. It was through prayer that I truly felt the healing touch of God. Pouring my heart out to the divine—sharing my fears, doubts, and pain—brought a sense of peace and release that I had never experienced before.

It was as if a weight had been lifted, replaced with a sense of hope and renewed purpose. This journey of confronting the shadows, seeking forgiveness, and finding healing wasn't a sprint but a marathon. It took time, effort, and a willingness to embrace vulnerability.

With each step, I grew stronger, more resilient, and more confident in my faith. Looking back, I realize that the darkness I faced wasn't meant to destroy me; it was meant to reveal the depth of God's love, the power of forgiveness, and the transformative strength of faith. It was a journey that led me to a place of healing, redemption, and ultimately, to a life transformed by grace.

# The Strength of Perseverance

The journey of faith is not always a smooth road. It's a path filled with twists and turns, obstacles, and challenges that test our resolve and challenge our beliefs. But it's precisely in these moments of struggle, when darkness seems to engulf us, that the true strength of our faith is revealed. The journey is not about avoiding challenges but about enduring them with unwavering faith. Perseverance is not merely about gritting our teeth and pushing through.

It's about cultivating a deep trust in God, a belief that His plans for us are greater than we can comprehend. It's about holding fast to His promises, even when we feel lost, confused, or utterly alone. Perseverance is a choice, a deliberate act of faith, a conscious decision to trust in the unseen, to believe in the power of hope, even when our circumstances scream otherwise. Think of a mighty oak tree, standing tall against the fiercest storms. It's not just its sturdy trunk that allows it to withstand the winds and the rain, but its deep roots that anchor it firmly to the ground. Our faith is like those roots—invisible to the naked eye, yet powerful enough to sustain us through life's most challenging storms.

Remember, our faith is not just a concept or a belief system. It's a living, breathing force that empowers us to navigate life's challenges with courage and resilience. When we are tempted to give up, to surrender to the darkness, we must remember the promises of God, the strength He provides, and the hope He offers. The journey of faith is not a sprint but a marathon. There will be times when we feel exhausted, discouraged, and ready to quit. But just as a marathon runner pushes through the pain to reach the finish line, we must hold onto our faith and keep going, trusting that God will sustain us every step of the way. The strength of perseverance is not a magic trick, nor is it a secret formula.

It's about choosing faith over fear, hope over despair, and believing in the power of God's grace to carry us through. It's about embracing the journey, knowing that even in the darkest moments, there is always light, always hope, always a reason to keep going. And when we do—when we persevere through the storms and emerge on the other side—we will find that our faith has been strengthened, our character refined, and our spirit renewed. We will have grown in ways we never imagined, our capacity for love and compassion deepened, and our understanding of God's grace expanded.

The strength of perseverance is not just about enduring challenges; it's about transforming them, using them as opportunities for growth, deepening our faith, and drawing us closer to God. It's about emerging from the fire not just unscathed, but refined, purified, and even more radiant than before. So let us embrace the journey, with all its twists and turns, its joys and sorrows, its triumphs and setbacks. Let us persevere, trusting in God's faithfulness, His love, and His unending grace. For in the end, it is not the journey itself, but the strength of our faith that will define us. And that strength, my friends, is a force that can move mountains, heal brokenness, and transform lives. It's a power that can change the world, one heart, one life, one act of unwavering faith at a time.

# A Life Unraveled

As I navigated my teenage years, my faith became an increasingly important anchor in my life, especially after the passing of my beloved grandfather. His death left a profound impact on me, and it was during this difficult time that I found solace in my church community and my relationship with God. I threw myself into my studies and graduated in 1991, ready to embark on a new chapter of my life. Little did I know that this chapter would involve not only marriage but also entrepreneurship. My wife and I worked tirelessly side by side, building our business from the ground up.

It was challenging yet rewarding, and I met a myriad of interesting characters along the way—some who offered a helping hand and others who presented obstacles. Despite the long hours and sacrifices, I knew that my hard work was paving the way for a brighter future. During this time, I also cherished the role of being the oldest sibling to my three younger sisters. I took on the responsibility of looking out for them, especially since our childhood had involved frequent moves and changes. I wanted to be a stable presence in their lives, someone they could rely on.

With the business came travel to different trade shows and late nights spent around the wrong crowd—the kind of people who always seem to want something from you. You probably know some like that, and it's not a good influence at all. I found myself going down the wrong path. It took years to realize this—it didn't happen overnight, believe me. When I say you become who you hang around with, it's true. And, at that time, God wasn't in my life as He had been before. Perhaps I was angry over the loss of my grandfather; I'm not entirely sure.

# The Shadow Creeping In

As I continued striving to build my own business, fate struck once again on August 8, 1998, when I was just 26 years old. The weight of my responsibilities hit me hard as I received the devastating news that my 14-year-old sister, Ashley, had been killed just a mile away from our parents' house. Despite my disbelief, I knew I had to step up and face the harsh reality. Never did I imagine that I would be arranging a funeral for my beloved sister at such a young age. I remember arriving at my parents' house to find our pastor and my mom, who was sitting in her chair, consumed by grief.

It was then that I realized the unimaginable truth—it was Ashley who was no longer with us. I walked out of the house and leaned against my truck, trying to make sense of it all. My father came out, and the only thing he could say was, "I don't know how I'm going to afford this." In that moment, I reassured him that I would take care of everything, not fully comprehending what I was getting myself into. The next day, I had my first encounter with what I believe were God's angels.

My father was frantically searching through Ashley's room, desperately looking for a Mickey Mouse watch he had given her. When I asked him what he was doing, he explained his mission. After he came up empty-handed, I went to the crash site and joined in the search. Suddenly, a man appeared and asked what we were looking for. After I explained, he dropped to his knees and searched alongside me. Within minutes, a woman dressed in all white appeared and offered her assistance. As we turned to her, she handed me the watch, still ticking despite the broken pin on its band.

With a brief message, she disappeared, followed by the man who had helped me, leaving me in awe of what I had just experienced. That was the first of many encounters I had with what I believe were angels sent to guide me through the difficult times ahead. I have always felt their presence, knowing they were there to help me cope with the challenges that lay ahead.

They gave me the strength to take care of my grieving parents, a task I would never wish upon anyone. As time passed, I couldn't help but remember their faces and that day. However, the pain and burden of losing my sister didn't fully register with me. I never truly mourned her passing. I felt myself drifting away from what I knew, unable to find my way through the widening fork in the road. I tried to create my own path, but I stopped going to church and even skipped holiday services. Deep down, I may have been angry at God for taking her at such a young age, but I knew in my heart that she was in a better place in heaven. Yet, the anger and hurt lingered.

Life went on for me, and I eventually had two children of my own. As they grew older, I couldn't help but see my sister's face in my daughter's. I found myself surrounded by the wrong people and engaging in destructive behaviors. I got divorced, realizing that I had married too young and without truly knowing myself. Then, life seemed to spiral out of control. I was on a roller coaster, crashing and crashing again. More loved ones passed away, and I became numb to the cycles of life and death. I felt like I was just existing, taking up space in this world. The shadow began to creep in slowly, almost imperceptibly at first.

Like a creeping vine, it started with tendrils of doubt, anxieties that coiled around my mind, whispering insidious lies that chipped away at my foundation. It was subtle at first—a nagging worry, an inexplicable dread that clung to me like a shroud. The events that triggered this descent into despair were not singular cataclysmic events but rather a series of small, seemingly insignificant incidents that gradually unraveled the tapestry of my life. The once-bright colors of my aspirations began to fade into muted tones of gray. My dreams, once vibrant and alive, became brittle and fragile, easily shattered by the relentless winds of pessimism. What had once fueled my passion, my desire to make a difference, now felt like a distant memory, replaced by an overwhelming sense of weariness and apathy. The seeds of doubt were planted long ago, taking root in the fertile soil of my insecurities. The whispers of self-criticism grew louder, morphing into a deafening chorus of negativity that drowned out any semblance of self-worth.

I became my own worst enemy, a relentless critic of my own inadequacies, magnifying every flaw and minimizing every accomplishment. My life took a devastating turn when my mother was diagnosed with cancer at the young age of 58. Just a few days later, my brother-in-law fell ill, and I couldn't help but wonder why all of this was happening. It felt like the universe was constantly throwing challenges at me, and I couldn't help but feel angry. As my mother and brother-in-law started chemotherapy, I couldn't help but admire their strength and resilience. They were both incredible individuals who never gave up, and I truly believe that my brother-in-law's support played a huge role in their journey.

But amidst all of this, I found myself in a relationship where no one seemed to care about my well-being. As long as I provided for them, everything was fine. My mother was a ten-year cancer survivor, and I couldn't have been more grateful. But as her health deteriorated, I felt like the walls were closing in on me. I knew that if I just prayed and trusted in God, He would guide me through this difficult time. But my stubbornness got in the way, and I struggled to find solace. Then, in November 2021, my mother was diagnosed with leukemia and given only 30 days to live. And to make matters worse, this was right in the middle of the COVID pandemic.

While we were at the hospital, both my brother-in-law, sister, and I contracted the virus, despite taking all necessary precautions. We managed to bring my mother home on hospice, but the very next day, all three of us were sick. By Monday, I was so weak that I couldn't even walk and had to seek medical help. The doctor told me that I needed to be hospitalized, but I stubbornly refused. For the next three and a half weeks, I was at home, struggling with my illness and knowing that my mother's health was rapidly declining. I lost 47 pounds during this nightmare, and I regret not being able to spend more time with my mother in her final days. But I did manage to be by her side for a few days before she passed away on December 8, 2021, at 7:47 pm, with my sisters and father by her side.

As I stood there, thinking things couldn't possibly get any worse, they did. I stepped outside into the cold night to call my children and deliver the heartbreaking news that their grandmother had passed away.

As I explained, my daughter's response was met with a loud thud as the phone hit the floor. I was overcome with shock, and the next thing I remember was being in my truck, shivering and disoriented. The flashing lights of an ambulance and my father's concerned presence next to me were the only things I could make out. The EMTs urged me to go to the hospital, warning that my body was shutting down from shock. I couldn't believe this was happening; I should have been there beside my father. But he calmly spoke, telling me he needed the distraction for a moment to take his mind off Mom, if only for a moment. As the day progressed, with the funeral and calling hours ahead, a song called "Scars in Heaven" was sent to me.

I had never heard it before, but that night I listened to it on repeat. I knew I had to sing this song at my mom's funeral. By the grace of God, it was the only way I was going to get through it (a lesson I learned later on). December has always been a difficult month to navigate, especially with the loss of a loved one. But I want you to know that you can get through it. Hold on to hope and remember that you are not alone. The world around me seemed to lose its vibrancy, its colors fading into a monotone of gray.

The things that once brought joy and laughter now felt dull and lifeless. My hobbies, once a source of solace and distraction, became tedious and mundane, offering no escape from the suffocating grip of despair. Every day became a struggle, a monotonous cycle of exhaustion and emptiness. The simplest tasks, like getting out of bed or showering, felt like insurmountable obstacles. My body, once a vessel of vitality, now felt heavy and burdened, weighed down by the unrelenting weight of despair. The shadows that had once lingered on the periphery of my consciousness began to consume me, engulfing me in a darkness that seemed impenetrable. It felt as if I was drowning in a sea of hopelessness, the surface of hope vanishing beneath the relentless waves of negativity. In those bleakest moments, I found myself questioning the very meaning of existence.

Why?

Why endure this relentless pain?

The whispers of despair, once faint and distant, now echoed in my ears, taunting me with the allure of oblivion.

I began to entertain thoughts I had never dared to consider before—thoughts that sent shivers down my spine and knotted my stomach in a vice-like grip of dread. The abyss of despair was a terrifying place, a desolate wasteland where hope withered and dreams died. It was a place where the weight of the world felt unbearable, and the future seemed bleak and hopeless. In those darkest moments, I felt completely alone, a solitary figure adrift in a vast sea of emptiness. My descent into despair was a gradual process, a slow and insidious unraveling of my soul. But as the darkness deepened, so did the desperation, until it reached a point where I could no longer bear the unbearable. I felt trapped, as if I was in a relentless freefall, hurtling toward a precipice I could not escape.

# The Brink of Oblivion

Days bled into nights, each moment a torturous extension of the previous. I found myself trapped in a vortex of negative thoughts, a relentless loop of self-deprecation and self-recrimination. It was as if a voice within me—dark and insidious—whispered lies, constantly reminding me of my inadequacies, my failures, and my worthlessness. I had become my own worst enemy, a relentless critic of every thought, every action, every breath.

Sleep offered no escape. My nights were haunted by nightmares, vivid and terrifying, mirroring the turmoil that raged within. The darkness seemed to seep into my very being, chilling me to the bone, stealing every ounce of warmth and hope that had once sustained me. I retreated further into myself, seeking solace in the cold embrace of solitude—a desperate attempt to escape the torment that plagued me. The world around me faded into a blurry, meaningless backdrop. The vibrant hues of life, once so captivating, now seemed drained of color, reduced to a monotonous gray canvas.

Sounds, once a symphony of life, were now mere echoes—distant and hollow—reflecting the emptiness that consumed me. The laughter of children, the chirping of birds, the gentle rustling of leaves—all seemed to mock my misery, a stark contrast to the silent symphony of my inner torment. The burden of existence had grown unbearably heavy. I was weary, physically and emotionally drained. Every fiber of my being screamed for release, for an end to the unrelenting agony that had become my reality. The thought of suicide, once a distant and horrifying notion, now whispered temptingly in the darkest corners of my mind. It promised an escape, a release from the unbearable pain that had become my constant companion.

The thought, once terrifying, began to hold a morbid allure. It offered a sense of control, a way to finally silence the torment that raged within. The idea of ending the pain, of simply ceasing to exist, became an irresistible siren song, beckoning me toward its dark embrace.

As the new year began, I reflected on the past few months and the toll they had taken on me with their constant ups and downs. From relationships to my mother's sickness, I felt drained and unable to focus on work. Then, in July of 2022, I found myself driving, and before I knew it, I had crossed the state line into Florida. I knew I had to stop somewhere along the way, living in Indiana, but I couldn't remember where. So, I continued on to Daytona Beach. When I arrived, it was storming, with lightning flashing across the sky.

Despite the weather, I parked my vehicle and walked to the beach, where the waves crashed, and the rain poured down. The wind howled, and I walked out into the ocean, chest deep. In that moment, I thought that my death would look like an accident and that no one would care. But as I gazed out across the vast ocean, I saw Jesus walking towards me, calling me by name. It was as if I was in a trance as he spoke, his voice both commanding and soothing. He said, "Robert, it's not your time. Turn around and go back." I stood there, frozen in time, but eventually, I turned and walked back to the beach. As I made my way back onto the shore, I turned to look back at the ocean. To my surprise, the water was smooth as glass, and the storm had disappeared.

The stars twinkled above, and the moon shone brighter than I had ever seen before. It was a moment that left a deep impact on my soul, reminding me that there is always hope and guidance, even in the midst of the darkest storms. After venturing out for the night, I found a room to rest in. The next morning, I woke up early and decided to take a stroll. As I made my way to the patio pool area, a man suddenly appeared on my left and placed his arm around me. He shared that he had been in a similar place as I was and urged me to sit down for a conversation. Feeling a bit wary, I responded curtly, stating that I did not know him. But he confidently replied, "You will get to know me."

His name was Seth, and he hailed from Atlanta, Georgia. Despite my initial reservations, I indulged him and sat down to talk. We spent hours conversing, learning about each other's journeys. As I got up to leave, Seth told me to meet him at the same spot the next morning. I hesitated, explaining that I had no idea where I would be. But he assured me, "I do. You will be right here." As I walked along the beach that day, reflecting on my conversation with a stranger, I couldn't help but wonder what was wrong with me. That evening, I returned to my room with a bad sunburn. The next morning, I woke up and headed outside, only to find Seth waiting for me at the same spot. As we talked, a woman approached us and kissed Seth on the head, telling him to take all the time he needed. She then walked away, and Seth beamed, revealing that she had saved his life at that very spot seven years ago.

He shared his story of trying to end his life and how this place had become a turning point for him. I ended up spending the entire day on the beach with Seth and the woman. As the day turned into night, I couldn't help but reflect on the events of the past three days. I realized that God had intervened in my life in a powerful way, placing someone who had gone through a similar struggle in my path. And that person, along with God, had been there when no one else was.

My thoughts were racing—was I right? Did I need help? I kept asking myself if I needed to go to the hospital. I sought out information, delving into the darkest corners of the internet, seeking solace in the knowledge that I was not alone in my despair. The anonymity of the digital world allowed me to explore the depths of my darkness without the fear of judgment. I found solace in the shared stories of others who had experienced similar darkness, finding a twisted sense of camaraderie in their shared suffering.

But amidst the darkness, a faint glimmer of hope flickered. It wasn't a sudden revelation, but a subtle shift in my internal landscape. A whisper of doubt, a hesitant questioning of the path I was on. My mind, for the first time in what felt like an eternity, began to resist the pull of despair. It was a fleeting moment, a fragile spark in the abyss of my despair, but it was enough. It wasn't a sudden epiphany but a slow, agonizing process of unraveling the layers of pain that had encased me.

Like a cocoon emerging from its chrysalis, I felt myself slowly beginning to break free from the bonds of self-destruction. The darkness that had consumed me for so long began to recede, replaced by a faint, fragile glimmer of hope. I reached out for help. It was a monumental step, a terrifying leap of faith. But the faint flicker of hope that had emerged within me emboldened me to seek solace, to acknowledge my vulnerability and reach out for the lifeline I desperately needed.

As the days passed, I found myself mowing the grass and listening to music, as I always do when on the mower. Suddenly, "Amazing Grace" started playing, and it hit me like a ton of bricks. I knew I needed to invite Jesus Christ into my heart and seek forgiveness for my sins. Right there in the middle of the field, I turned to Him for help. I learned that no matter what I had done, I could ask for forgiveness and believe in Jesus' sacrifice on the cross for our sins. It was an incredible feeling.

As a slow learner, it took me some time to fully understand, but I was starting to figure it out. In the following days and weeks, I reached out to a couple of pastors—one from the church I grew up in and another I had met a few years back. One Sunday, right before service, a man approached me and asked if he could sit next to me in the pew. To my surprise, it was my former youth pastor, who now walked with a cane. I gladly slid over to make room for him, and we sat through the service together. Afterwards, he told me that the pastor had shared some information about what I had been going through.

He then opened up to me about his own struggles, revealing that he had once tried to end his life due to the unbearable pain from a back injury. However, just as he was about to carry out his plan, his phone rang, and his boss told him to go home and rest. It was another sign to him that God was involved in his life.

Here was a man who I had always looked up to and respected as a good Christian, and yet he too had faced such deep struggles. It made me realize that the ones who suffer the most are often the ones left behind with unanswered questions—not the ones who take their own lives. I couldn't help but think that God was trying to tell me something, but I wasn't sure what it was or if I was truly listening. All I knew was that I was determined to figure it out.

I recently encountered an individual through dating, and I wish I had seen through their façade from the beginning because things did not turn out well. They professed to attend church and shared their plans with me, but it was all a lie. When it came time to actually go, they always had an excuse—from not having anything to wear to not feeling well. I heard every excuse imaginable. Before I knew it, I was missing out on going to church, something that I wanted and needed to do.

My good friend and sister saw that I was going backwards and advised me to distance myself from this individual. It was a difficult process, as I was mentally exhausted from all the excuses. But with God's help, I finally managed to break free. I continued to pray and put my faith and trust in Him, not knowing where I would end up. Through this experience, I have had the opportunity to share with others about what Jesus has done for me. One gentleman asked me about my knowledge of Jesus, and I have also spoken with others who were contemplating suicide. What I have learned is that Jesus is the way, no matter what you have done or think. He loves you unconditionally. He may not answer your prayers immediately, and it may not be in the exact way you hoped for, but He knows what we truly need before we even ask.

All you have to do is open your heart and let Him in. It will be worth it, I promise. As I continue to pray and seek Jesus, He has brought an incredible, loving, and understanding woman into my life. She believes in His power and knows that all things are possible through Him. Together, we are more powerful with Him by our side. Jesus knew that I needed her and sent her to me. One important lesson I have learned from her is that a relationship is not 40/60 or 20/80; it is 100/100. We should always give our all, and when one of us is down, the other can lift them up. Jesus wants us to have a partner in life who shares our faith and helps us grow closer to Him.

In Genesis 2:18, God declares that it is not beneficial for a man to be alone; therefore, He created a suitable companion for him. It is imperative to have the assistance of one's spouse in order to effectively lead one's household. Allow me to encourage you to not lose hope, to remain steadfast, and to trust in Jesus' provision. Remember, you are not alone, even if it may feel like it. Don't hesitate to pray, speak up, and seek help when needed.

It's possible that those closest to you, such as a friend, family member, or colleague, have also struggled with suicidal thoughts. Sometimes, simply talking and listening to someone else can make a significant difference. There are many available resources that I will include at the end. This is a frightening health emergency that can be overwhelming for both you and your loved ones, evoking a range of emotions such as sadness, fear, and anger. However, it is important to remember that you are always cherished by Jesus and your family, regardless of your actions or thoughts. The healing journey is unique for each individual and requires time. I may not be an expert, but I have personally experienced and survived through this. I am sharing my story in the hope that if you find yourself in this situation, you will turn to prayer and seek support from your family, friends, and organizations.

It is also crucial to consider how this would impact your family and children, as they are the ones who will truly suffer if someone takes their own life. The journey was far from effortless. My path to healing was filled with challenges, setbacks, and moments of hopelessness that threatened to drag me back into the depths. But with each small step, I could feel myself getting closer to the light. The darkness that once consumed me began to retreat, replaced by a newfound appreciation for life and the simple pleasures that had been lost in the chaos of my anguish. I sought out the support of friends, family, and faith-based communities. Their love and encouragement, their willingness to listen without judgment, provided a lifeline during the darkest moments. I learned to be vulnerable, to share my pain without fear of rejection, to allow myself to be loved and supported. Most importantly, I found myself drawn to the solace of faith, to the words of hope and redemption that whispered through the pages of scripture.

The comfort I found in prayer, in the assurance of a loving God who cared for me, even in my darkest moments, became my anchor, my guide through the storm. It wasn't a magic bullet, but a steady beacon of hope, a promise of a future beyond my despair. It was a long and painful journey, a process of peeling back layers of pain, grief, and self-destruction. But with each step, with each moment of vulnerability, with each whisper of prayer, I felt myself inching closer to the light.

The darkness that had once consumed me began to fade, replaced by a newfound appreciation for life, for the simple joys that had been lost in the chaos of my despair. The journey wasn't over. There would be moments of struggle, of doubt, of temptation to return to the comforting embrace of darkness. But I knew that I was not alone. I had found a community of support, a source of strength in faith, and a love that transcended the boundaries of my own despair. I was still grappling with the scars of my past, but the darkness no longer held me captive. I had found a path to redemption, a source of hope that illuminated the darkest corners of my soul. And in that hope, I discovered a newfound purpose, a reason to live, a reason to fight for a future filled with light, love, and the promise of a life transformed.

# A Cry for Help

For those attempting to assist someone struggling with suicidal thoughts or actions, it is important to inquire about how you can help. Pray with them and remember the incomparable power of Jesus Christ. Take steps to secure and remove any potentially harmful items, such as firearms or medication, and encourage them to speak with a therapist, doctor, pastor, or trusted friends.

Emphasize the importance of a healthy diet, regular exercise, and adequate sleep in aiding their recovery. Work together to identify ways to support their healing and become familiar with available resources. This approach can have a profound impact.

# The Silence of the Void

S o how do we practice empathy in our daily lives? First, we must be willing to listen—really listen. Not with the intention to respond or to judge, but with the intention to understand. Put aside our own thoughts and opinions and truly focus on the words of the other person.

Second, we must be willing to ask questions. When we ask questions, we show that we care and are genuinely interested in understanding their experience. We must ask with humility and curiosity, seeking to learn and grow. Third, we must be willing to validate their feelings. It's not about agreeing with their perspective but about acknowledging that their emotions are valid. Let them know that you hear them, that you understand their pain, that you care.

Fourth, we must be willing to offer support. This might mean simply being present, offering a listening ear, or providing practical assistance. It's about showing that you are there for them, that you are in their corner, that you care. Fifth, we must be willing to forgive. Holding onto anger and resentment only hurts us in the long run. Forgiveness is not about condoning the actions of others; it's about releasing ourselves from the chains of bitterness. It's about choosing to let go of the pain and move forward.

As Christians, empathy is not just a nice thing to do; it's a commandment. Jesus said, "Love your neighbor as yourself" (Matthew 22:39). How can we truly love our neighbor if we don't understand their pain? How can we truly love our neighbor if we don't see the world through their eyes? Empathy is the foundation of a compassionate society. It's the key to building bridges, fostering understanding, and creating a world where everyone feels seen, heard, and valued. It's a gift we can all give, and it's a gift that can change the world.

So let's choose empathy. Let's choose to see the world through the eyes of others, to understand their pain, and to offer them our love and support. Let's be the hands and feet of Jesus, bringing His love and compassion into a world that desperately needs it.

As you read these words, I encourage you to reflect on your own life. How can you practice empathy more fully? Where can you show compassion to those around you? What are the small, simple ways you can make a difference in the lives of others? Remember, it doesn't take grand gestures to make a difference. Sometimes, the smallest acts of kindness can have the greatest impact. A smile, a listening ear, a helping hand—all of these can be expressions of empathy and compassion. Let us choose to live lives filled with empathy, compassion, and love. Let us be a light in the darkness, a beacon of hope, and a reminder that God's love is always available to those who need it.

# The Promise of Redemption

T he promise of redemption, woven deeply into the fabric of Christianity, became my lifeline, my beacon in the abyss of despair. It was a concept that had always been there, a whisper in the back of my mind, but it was only through my personal encounter with Jesus that it became a tangible truth. Redemption, in its essence, speaks of restoration, cleansing, and a second chance—a complete reversal of the devastating effects of sin and its consequences. It's a message of hope that cuts through the darkness, a powerful affirmation that no matter how deep the chasm, no matter how overwhelming the pain, there's always a path back to light.

The very idea of redemption had been a distant echo in my life, a concept I barely grasped, let alone embraced. My path had been marred by choices driven by a relentless internal storm that seemed to have no end. I was lost in a labyrinth of self-destruction, haunted by the ghosts of my past mistakes. The weight of my actions pressed down on me with crushing force, drowning me in a sea of self-condemnation.

But then came that moment—the moment when I finally surrendered, when I realized I was powerless to break free on my own. It was the moment when I cried out for a power greater than myself, a power that could heal the wounds that festered within, a power that could offer forgiveness and restoration.

It was in that moment that I met Jesus—not in a grand, orchestrated display, but in a simple, quiet encounter that shifted the course of my life forever. The promise of redemption was not a fleeting idea, a mere concept that faded with the changing tides. It was a profound truth that resonated within my being, a truth that permeated every fiber of my existence. It was the very foundation upon which my healing and transformation were built. It was the promise that lifted me out of the depths of despair, the promise that carried me through the stormy seas of life.

This promise, this hope of redemption, did not negate the reality of my past, my mistakes, or the consequences that followed. It didn't erase the pain, the hurt, or the scars that marked my journey. It did not diminish the weight of my choices. But what it did do was offer me a way forward—a path to healing and a promise of a life transformed. It offered forgiveness, not as a cheap dismissal of my wrongdoings, but as a profound act of grace, a love that reached into the depths of my brokenness and offered me a fresh start.

The promise of redemption was not just a personal promise, whispered in the stillness of my heart. It was a universal promise, a promise available to anyone, transcending the boundaries of time, culture, and circumstance. It extended to the lost and broken, those who had stumbled and fallen, and those burdened by the weight of their own choices. It whispered, "You are not alone. There is hope. There is forgiveness. There is a way back."

Redemption is a powerful force, a force that can shatter the chains of guilt and shame, a force that can restore the shattered pieces of a broken heart. It's a force that can empower us to walk into a future, not defined by our past, but by the hope and love we embrace. It's a force that can turn the tide of despair into a current of hope, carrying us towards a life that reflects the grace and mercy we have received.

The promise of redemption is not a passive promise that we merely receive and then forget. It's a promise that demands action, a promise that calls us to step into a new life characterized by gratitude, forgiveness, and a commitment to living a life that reflects the love and grace we have been given. The promise of redemption compels us to reach out to others, to offer them the same grace and hope we have received. It calls us to be agents of change, to share the light of redemption with a world in need. It challenges us to walk into our own destiny, using our experiences to heal and empower, building bridges of compassion and understanding in a world often divided and broken.

Redemption is a gift, a precious gift that we must not take for granted. It calls us to live a life of purpose, a life that honors the love we have received, a life that reflects the grace and mercy that have set us free. It calls us to live a life of hope, a life that embraces the promise of a future filled with possibilities.

So, if you find yourself struggling, if you feel burdened by the weight of your past, remember the promise of redemption. Remember that there is a power greater than yourself that offers a path to healing, a path to restoration, a path to a life transformed. Reach out, embrace the promise, and walk into the future that awaits, filled with the hope and love that can only come from a heart redeemed.

# The Unlikely Encounter

The power of my testimony is something I've come to appreciate more and more over the years. It wasn't something I initially sought out—the idea of sharing my story with others felt both terrifying and unnecessary. I was so caught up in my own struggles, my own pain, that I couldn't imagine how my story could be of any value to anyone else. But then, something unexpected happened. I started to receive messages from people who had heard me speak about my journey.

They shared their own struggles, their own feelings of despair and hopelessness, and in their stories, I saw reflections of my own pain. It was in those moments, witnessing the shared humanity of our struggles, that I truly understood the power of my testimony. My story wasn't just about me—it was a story of hope, redemption, and the transformative power of faith. And for those who were grappling with similar challenges, it offered a glimmer of light in the darkness, a whisper of hope that they weren't alone.

In the depths of my despair, I felt completely isolated, like my pain was unique and unbearable. But as I began to share my story, I discovered a profound truth: our struggles, in many ways, are universal. We all experience pain, loss, doubt, and despair. We all yearn for connection, for love, for hope. And it is in sharing our stories, our vulnerabilities, our journeys of faith and healing, that we create a bridge of understanding, a space of empathy, a beacon of hope that can illuminate the darkest of paths. There's a beautiful verse in the Bible, Psalm 18:2, that speaks to this very truth: "The Lord is my rock, my fortress, and my deliverer; my God is my rock, in whom I take refuge, my shield and the horn of my salvation, my stronghold."

This verse resonated with me deeply during my darkest hours. It painted a powerful image of God as a stronghold, a refuge, a source of unwavering strength and protection. It offered me solace in the face of fear, hope amidst despair, and a reminder that even in the darkest moments, I was not alone.

I remember sitting in a dimly lit room, consumed by the overwhelming weight of my pain, feeling like I was drowning in a sea of despair. I had given up on everything and everyone. I had convinced myself that there was no hope, no possibility of healing, no reason to continue living. But then, I stumbled upon this verse, and a flicker of hope ignited within me. It was a small spark, but it was enough. It was enough to remind me that even in the darkest of times, God was with me. He was my refuge, my shield, my protector.

And as I clung to this hope, I began to find my way back to the light. Sharing my story, my journey of faith and recovery, has become a way for me to offer that same spark of hope to others. It's a way to remind them that they are not alone, that their pain is not unique, that there is hope for healing, for redemption, for a new beginning. Each time I share my testimony, I see the light of hope reflected in the eyes of those listening. I see the flicker of recognition, the quiet nod of understanding, the unspoken connection that transcends words. It's a powerful reminder that we are all part of a larger story, a tapestry of humanity woven together by the shared experiences of life, love, loss, and faith.

My testimony is not about boasting or self-promotion. It's not about showcasing my strength or downplaying my struggles. It's about being a beacon of hope, a reminder that even in the darkest of moments, even when it feels like there's no way out, there's always hope. There's always the possibility of redemption, of healing, of finding our way back to the light. And that hope, that possibility, that transformative power, lies in our shared humanity, in our willingness to connect, to listen, to share our stories, and to offer each other the grace, forgiveness, and love we all need to heal, to grow, and to find our way back to the light.

# The Light in the Darkness

The whispers of hope that began to fill my heart after my encounter with Jesus continued to grow stronger with each passing day. It was like a seed, planted in the fertile ground of my soul, that was slowly but surely pushing its way through the hardened crust of despair. The light of faith, once a distant glimmer, had become a beacon guiding me through the darkness. I started to feel a sense of peace I hadn't known before. The constant gnawing anxiety that had plagued me for so long seemed to subside, replaced by a quiet calm that filled my being.

I began to see the world through a different lens, no longer clouded by the despair and hopelessness that had consumed me. My perspective shifted, and I started to notice the beauty and goodness that had always been present, but I had been too blinded to see. It wasn't a sudden transformation but a gradual awakening. The darkness still lingered, but I felt a growing strength to face it, a newfound resilience that stemmed from the hope I had found in Christ. It was as if the weight of my burdens had been lifted, replaced by a sense of lightness and freedom I had never before experienced.

The journey of healing wasn't without its challenges. There were days when the shadows of my past threatened to engulf me once again, but I found strength in the promises of God. I discovered the power of prayer, a direct line of communication with the divine, where I could pour out my fears, doubts, and anxieties, and find solace and comfort in His presence. I also found solace in the scriptures, the words of life that offered guidance, encouragement, and hope. The stories of people who had endured unimaginable hardships, yet remained steadfast in their faith, gave me strength and inspiration. I realized that I wasn't alone in my struggles and that countless others had found hope and redemption through faith. This realization was a turning point in my journey. It gave me a sense of purpose, a reason to fight for my recovery and overcome the obstacles that lay before me.

I started to see the potential for a new life, a life filled with meaning and purpose. The desire to live, which had been dormant for so long, was rekindled, fueled by the hope of a brighter future. I also recognized the importance of community. The isolation I had experienced during my darkest hours had only amplified my pain and despair. I realized that I needed the support and encouragement of others, particularly those who understood the struggles I was facing. I sought out a church community, a place where I could connect with others who shared my faith and who could offer me a sense of belonging and support.

The warmth and acceptance I found in this community were a balm to my wounded soul. It was a safe space where I could be myself, without judgment or shame. I found friends who listened to my story, who offered words of encouragement and support, and who helped me navigate the challenges of my recovery. The support I received from this community, coupled with my growing faith, gave me the strength to confront the shadows of my past. It wasn't an easy process. There were moments of pain, guilt, and regret, but with each step I took, I felt a sense of healing and release. I learned the importance of forgiveness, both for myself and for those who had hurt me.

This journey of healing was transformative, not only for my emotional and mental well-being but also for my spiritual life. I began to see the world through a different lens—a lens of love, compassion, and forgiveness. The darkness that had once consumed me was slowly fading, replaced by a light that shone from within. This new life I found in Christ was filled with a sense of purpose and meaning. It wasn't about escaping the challenges of life, but about facing them with faith and hope.

It was about finding strength in the midst of weakness, and joy in the midst of suffering. It was a journey that taught me that even in the darkest moments, there is always the possibility of a new beginning, a chance to find healing, hope, and redemption. It was a journey that showed me the transformative power of faith, the unwavering love of God, and the possibility of a life filled with joy, purpose, and meaning.

# Acknowledgments

This book would not have been possible without the unwavering support and encouragement of countless individuals. First and foremost, I want to thank my Lord and Savior, Jesus Christ. His grace, mercy, and unconditional love have been my constant companions throughout my journey, carrying me through the darkest of times and guiding me toward the light.

To my wife, Michelle, who has not judged me and has helped guide me closer to Jesus with her loving embrace, knowing God put her here for me, and to my family, who have loved and supported me unconditionally: your prayers, encouragement, and unwavering belief in me have been a source of immense strength.

I am eternally grateful for your presence in my life. To the friends who stood by me, offered a listening ear, and held my hand during my darkest hours, I owe an immeasurable debt of gratitude. Your kindness and compassion have been a beacon of light in my life. To the countless mentors and spiritual leaders who have inspired, guided, and challenged me to grow in my faith, I am deeply grateful for your wisdom and guidance. To the readers, I pray that my story will offer you hope, strength, and inspiration. May you find solace in knowing that even in the deepest despair, God's love and grace are always available, and healing and redemption are always possible.

# Appendix

This appendix contains additional resources and information that may be helpful to readers on their journey of faith and recovery.

**Recommended Reading:** A list of books and articles that explore themes of faith, healing, and redemption.

**Faith-Based Organizations:** A directory of organizations that offer support and resources for individuals seeking to grow in their faith or overcome personal challenges.

**Prayer Resources:** A collection of prayers and scripture passages that can be helpful for individuals seeking guidance, comfort, and strength.

# Glossary

This glossary provides definitions for key terms used throughout the book.

**Redemption:** The act of being saved from sin and its consequences through the sacrifice of Jesus Christ.

**Faith:** Trust and belief in God and His promises.

**Hope:** A confident expectation of something good and desirable.

**Grace:** God's unmerited favor and love for humanity.

**Forgiveness:** The act of pardoning someone for an offense and releasing them from the debt.

**Healing:** The process of restoring physical, emotional, or spiritual well-being.

**Transformation:** The process of being changed into something new or different.

# References

**Bible** (King James Version)

**The Purpose Driven Life** by Rick Warren

**The Power of Now** by Eckhart Tolle

**The Shack** by William P. Young

**Man's Search for Meaning** by Viktor Frankl

# Author Biography

Robert is a passionate advocate for faith and personal growth. He has overcome significant challenges in his life and found hope and healing through his encounter with Jesus Christ. He is dedicated to sharing his story and offering encouragement to others who are struggling. Robert Strong lives with his family in Indiana and enjoys spending time camping, attending car shows, and hanging out with family.